The author and publishers would like to thank Monisha Patil-Arya for acting as a consultant on this book.

They would also like to thank Carol Gorringe, Magdalen Gorringe, Joya Bannerjee, Mita Bannerjee and Debi Bannerjee for their help and participation.

The author and publishers would like to thank Kavi Arya for supplying the photograph on page 3, the Ancient Art and Art Collection for supplying the additional photograph of Nataraja on page 4 (bottom left) and Bury and Ann Peerless for supplying the photograph of Krishna on page 17.

DANCE OF SHIVA

Pratima Mitchell

Photographs by Liba Taylor

Hamish Hamilton

London

It is a cold November afternoon and Mita is in a hurry to get to her dance lesson at Magdalen's house.

'Sorry I'm late,' she says when Magdalen opens the door. 'Debi hid my bag and wouldn't tell where it was. In the end I had to let her come with me.' Mita's four-year-old sister looks up, rather pleased with herself.

Mita and Magdalen are learning Bharata Natyam dance. Bharata Natyam is the oldest form of classical dance. Their teacher is Monisha Arya, a well known dancer in India. Monisha started to learn Bharata Natyam in Bombay when she was a little girl. To become a good performer it takes years of lessons and many hours of daily practice.

When Bharata Natyam dancing started, 2000 years ago, it used to be part of religious worship in the temples of South India. Dancing was seen as a form of prayer to the gods, especially Shiva.

Before they start their lesson Monisha's pupils fold their hands and bow to their guru, or teacher. Then they say a prayer to Nataraja, the god of dance. If you look carefully you will see a small statue of Nataraja on the mantelpiece. Nataraja is another name for Shiva and he is often shown dancing in a circle which stands for the wheel of life.

Every lesson begins in the same way. Mita and Magdalen dance the first steps called *Tatti Khumbidal*. They are begging Mother Earth to forgive them for stamping on her.

Then they touch Monisha's feet as a sign of respect, because she is their guru.

Throughout the lesson Monisha taps out the rhythm with her rod on the block of wood called a *tattu-kali*. She also chants the beat out loud, 'Thayum That Ta, Thayum That Ta'. The girls join in. It helps them keep time.

Mita and Magdalen can't help giggling when they get some of the steps wrong, but Monisha can be quite stern with them. She makes them repeat the same steps over and over again, getting faster all the time.

Their movements have to be precise and in exact time to the beat. They try to concentrate hard and make them flowing and graceful as well.

Monisha watches them closely, following every detail of their movements and facial expressions. From time to time she stops them and corrects something.

After about half an hour of hard work Mita is beginning to get tired. Monisha tries to correct the line of her pose.
'Lift your arm higher. Is it falling asleep or what?'

Mita doesn't like being told off. She thinks she is doing her best. Sometimes Mita wishes Bharata Natyam wasn't such hard work. Her arms and legs ache all over. When Monisha dances it looks so effortless.

'You can't have that attitude,' says Monisha. 'When I was with my guru in Bombay I had to be careful never to seem to be cheeky. He would just have stopped teaching me. Why don't you sit down and have a rest?'

Mita cuddles Debi. Little sisters have their uses after all! Magdalen is trying the Nataraja pose. Can you see how it matches the little statue behind her? No, it's not quite right. Monisha straightens her hand and adjusts the angle of her arm. That looks better.

After her rest Mita joins Magdalen again to practise some of the basic steps, or *adavus*. They have to be very careful to get their hands and feet in the correct position. Everything has to be absolutely perfect.

'Look at me! I can do it too,'
cries Debi.
'Clever Debi,' says Mita. 'It won't be long before you can have dance lessons too.'

Mita and Magdalen know that there is a lot to learn to become good Bharata Natyam dancers. As well as all the movements, they have to know all the different gestures. In Bharata Natyam hand movements, or gestures, are used as a sort of sign language. With them a dancer can conjure up images of animals, landscape and people – or actions like eating, writing and sleeping.

Today Monisha is going to teach them some hand movements called *hastas*.

'Look closely,' she says. 'Can you make a fish?'
Monisha moves her hands from side to side to make the fish look as if it is swimming.

Here are some *hastas* for you to copy.

A fish.

A deer or a cow.

A lion with his mane.

A bee hovering over a lotus flower.

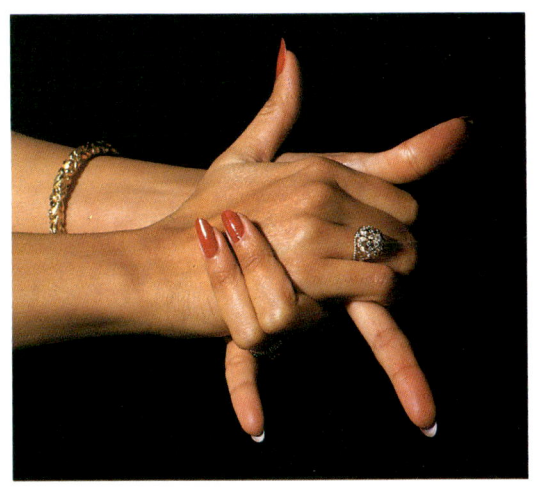

A tortoise.

A peacock.

'This is too difficult for me,' says Debi.
'Tuck in your third and fourth fingers like this,' Monisha demonstrates. Debi is planning to surprise her parents with her new skills. She can make a roaring lion with her hands.

In the middle of the lesson there is a phone call. '*Amma, adhuyaara?* Who is that, Mum?' Magdalen asks in Tamil. She still remembers the language she learned in South India where she used to live. Magdalen's mother sends her to call Monisha. 'It's Mrs Chopra from the Hindu Club,' she says.

Monisha returns with exciting news. 'The Ladies Cub want us to put on a short performance in a fortnight's time. Do you think we'll be able to get something ready by then?'

Magdalen is already thinking of ideas. There isn't really enough time to prepare a pure dance performance. 'Why don't we do a dance drama about Krishna when he was young?' she suggests.

Krishna is everyone's favourite Hindu god. He is often shown playing the flute, like in this picture. There are many stories and songs about him. He loved teasing his mother and the maidens who looked after the cows. Mita and Magdalen choose a story about Krishna when he was a naughty little boy.

In the story Krishna watches his mother putting some butter away in a cupboard. He steals it and when his mother comes back she finds the cupboard is empty. She asks Krishna if he took it but Krishna won't own up. Then she sees a smear of grease on his face. She knows he is the guilty one.

'There's a lot of work to be done,' says Monisha. All the movements and gestures will have to be learned, practised and perfected. They will also have to work hard to get the right facial expressions. In a dance drama the dancers have to tell the story through the dance.

Monisha shows Mita how to pretend to hide.
'Hold your hands like this,' she says. 'You have to imagine that you really are a cheeky little boy.'

Next Magdalen has to practise being his mother, Yashodha. She is questioning him and looking worried in a motherly sort of way.

When Krishna's mother accuses him of stealing the butter Mita pretends to look very innocent. Butter wouldn't melt in her mouth! Magdalen looks as if she sees through the pretence.

'Use your faces – your eyes and eybrows and mouths,' says Monisha. 'Try to feel what you are saying with your whole body.'

When the day of the performance arrives Monisha helps the girls to put on their make-up. Indian dancers use their eyes to make all sorts of expressions. A dark line of *kajal* is painted on to make the eyes look larger.

Mita wears a brilliant blue costume with a peacock feather in her hair. Krishna's colour is always blue and people say he used to wear a peacock feather in his hair.

Magdalen wears a pink sari and silver jewellery. She uses some fake golden hair to make her own blonde plait look even longer. In it she has woven some white flowers.

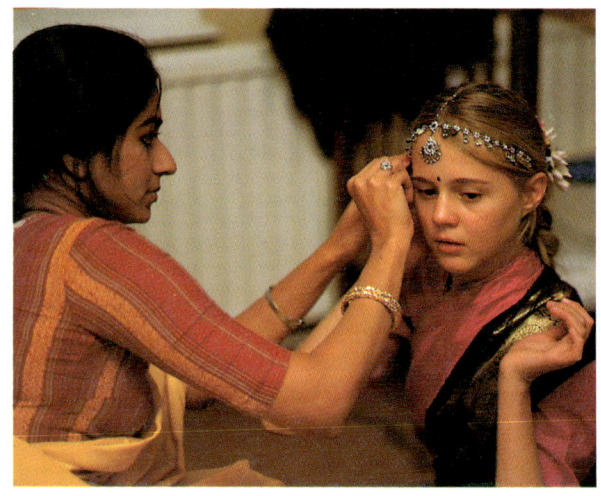

Mita's costume was specially made in South India. It is a 'stitched' sari with pantaloons and a little fan-shaped pleated frill in front. She wears a short, fitted blouse which ends at her midriff.

Magden has borrowed one of Monisha's most precious saris. She is quite nervous about wearing it.

Monisha ties on their 'ghungrus' or dancing bells. These are only ever worn for performances and they make a jingling noise when the dancers move.

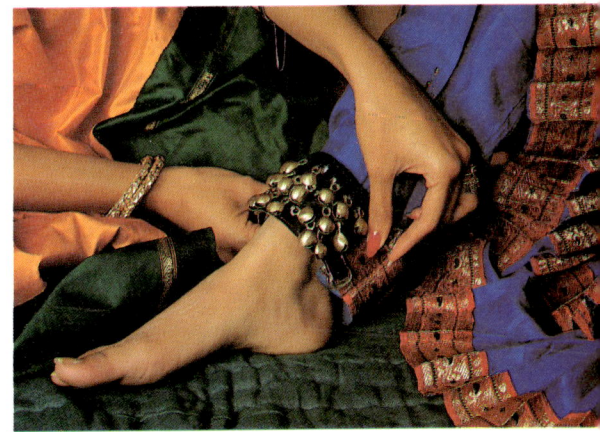

Their mouths feel dry and butterflies begin dancing in their stomachs when they see the audience waiting for the performance to begin. They don't want to disappoint them.

Krishna plays his flute and watches his mother put the butter in the cupboard. Mita follows Magdalen around the stage with her great big eyes.

When his mother has gone, naughty Krishna tiptoes up to the cupboard. He reaches up and finds the butter. All the time Mita keeps her body in a graceful pose. Look how carefully her feet are positioned.

Krishna thinks, 'Now's my chance.' He is eating the butter when he hears his mother coming back.

Now Magdalen has to act the stern parent.
'Have you seen the butter?' asks Krishna's mother.
'I know nothing about it,' he lies.

Mita and Magdalen are not allowed to speak. Using only gestures and facial expressions they tell the story to the audience.

Then Krishna's mother sees the tell-tale smear of grease on his face. 'Naughty boy,' she says. 'I shall punish you.'

Magdalen pretends to look very angry. Mita looks frightened. Even Krishna has to say sorry to his mother!

After the performance is over the girls relax with a cup of tea. They are pleased that everything went well. The audience clapped and clapped and they had to come back for a second bow.

'You did look cross,' says Mita. 'I thought you were going to push me right off the stage!'